*T*his book is dedicated
great alchemist, *Le Co*
his lifetime he was called
Europe. Today St. Germ

ascended master, a *P*urple *L*ight, who represents
universal victory, whose duty is to plant a victorious
seed in the soul of humanity. St. Germain has
revealed his secret *G*olden *A*lchemical *M*antra
to me. Without his gift, this work would have been
impossible.

# DIVINE AMBROSIA:
## HOW TO LIVE IN MIRACLES
### Great Alchemists' Secret Golden Alchemical Mantra

Recorded
By

Leia Gance, Ph. D.

*You are unlimited being, there is something out there waiting for your recognition.*

*Comte de St. Germain*

Bloomington, IN  Milton Keynes, UK

authorHOUSE

*AuthorHouse™*
*1663 Liberty Drive, Suite 200*
*Bloomington, IN 47403*
*www.authorhouse.com*
*Phone: 1-800-839-8640*

*AuthorHouse™ UK Ltd.*
*500 Avebury Boulevard*
*Central Milton Keynes, MK9 2BE*
*www.authorhouse.co.uk*
*Phone: 08001974150*

*First published by AuthorHouse 5/11/2006*

*ISBN: 1-4208-4756-2 (sc)*

*Printed in the United States of America*
*Bloomington, Indiana*

*This book is printed on acid-free paper.*

# $\mathcal{A}$CKNOWLEDGEMENTS

$\mathcal{V}$ery special thanks to Professor Jacob Pandian, Anthropologist, California State University, Fullerton, for his profound knowledge and genius. His magnificent personality and its power and breath encouraged me to break through to my inner spiritual being.

Another special thanks to all who participated in the evolution of*: DIVINE AMBROSIA: HOW TO LIVE IN MIRACLES—Great Alchemists' Secret Golden Alchemical Mantra* : Ms. Lucy Davis and her marvelous professional team, Mr. Dan Heise, Ms. Kathleen Burgess, Mrs. Rosemary Rapp, and Ms. Kinue Williams.

Very special thanks to my parents, Alan and Kate Gance, for their great love and support. They ceaselessly cared for and nurtured my soul throughout my life; their exemplary parenting helped me to see and to experience beauty in life.

Thanks a million to the members of Club Danzarin and to all my friends for invaluable support and love throughout.

Special thanks to Ms. Lynn Lewen, a friend who stood by me during the time of ordeal, with whose kindness remains with me for life.

Special thanks to Rev. Catherine Morris, metaphysician and mentor; her dedication towards her visionary work encouraged me to see another dimension of infinite possibility of the greater universe.

Finally, thanks a million to Laurence. In exhibiting his unique, ingenious mind, his meticulous and creative ideas in his worldview and his way of life, he has invited me into a new and unimaginable dimension. Without his support and lessons, the evolution of my inner being would not have unfolded this time.

# *Contents*

# $\mathcal{P}$REFACE: *The Secret of the Universe*

$I$ am compelled to explain what I have experienced. This experience is something that cannot be seen; it is beyond form. It can neither be heard because it is beyond sound nor can it be grasped; it is intangible. According to Tao, the supernatural phenomenal nature of the world is called indefinable and beyond imagination. I am attempting to illustrate St. Germain's "true existence" and his extraordinary information in this book. Perhaps it is as though, incomprehensible.

However, this "indefinable beyond imagination" has already been profoundly dissected, explored by ancient Greek philosophers. The nature of the universe is understood through an omnijective point of view of emanation, an inseparable concept of subjective and objective projection, which has been embraced throughout the ages. It is said in Tao, **"Just as the universe contains the 10,000 things: creatures, world, stars, so our mind contains 10,000 things, namely desires, impulses, fears, sensations, thoughts logically connected or not it serves them."** Thus, the mind is full of knowledge of the universe's contents. The Buddhist doctrine epitomizes which the universe is the larger body of God, and Man himself is the smaller body of God, but an equally wonderful habitation of the Divine being.

This concept has also been worshipped by Tantric philosophy, which is indispensable to the works of Alchemy and St. Germain's secret **G**olden **A**lchemical **M**antra. St. Germain insists that there is something much more to our mysterious universe, and with the help of his secret **GAM**, you can tap into these sources at this moment in life and witness its magnificence. It will prove to you its richness with unlimited abundance; all this can be yours if you do not resist the truth.

My mission is to emancipate Le Comte de St. Germain's message: *"Each of us were born with an inherent, unlimited potential (who realizes this truth) and you can be transformed into a being of 'there is nothing that is impossible. I will show you the way to access the transcendental path to the Divine Kingdom, the fountain of abundance."*

# PART I

# DIVINE AMBROSIA:
## HOW TO LIVE IN MIRACLES

## St. Germain's Secret Golden Alchemical Mantra

*As the Rays of the Sun Lighten and Glid the Blackest Cloud,
So the Soul by Entering the Body of the Universe Gives it Life and Immortality; the Ab ject it Lifts Up.*

*Plotinus*

# INTRODUCTION
## The Secret is Revealed

Man is a Microcosm, or a Little World,
Because He is an Extract From All the Stars
And Planets of the Whole Firmament,
From the Earth and the Elements;
And so He is Their Quintessence.

Paracelsus

*T*his secret Wisdom was bestowed upon
me by an eighteenth century alchemist, Le Comte
de St. Germain. During his lifetime, he was known
as a man of magnificent, unforgettable. Aside from
his well-known profile of transcendental being, he
is now widely known as an ascended master, Purple
Light, who represents universal victory, whose duty
is to plant a victorious seed in the soul of humanity.
(In the United States, he was introduced as Violet
Flame at the beginning of the twentieth century).
Purple Light is the most powerful healing light (fire)
that will transmute negative traits in the psycho/
physical department and can even penetrates into the

deeper level of subconscious realm to balance your outstanding karmic substances.

Ever since his departure from earth plain, Comte de St. Germain made contact with the people of various continents especially France, Germany, Scandinavia, and North America. He has assisted their life through prophetic messages. According to St. Germain, this secret **G**olden **A**lchemical **M**antra (one of the Alchemical Magic Ingredient within the St. Germain's Secret Alchemical Remedy which is revealed in my book of ***Great Alchemist and Quantum Manifestation Power: St. Germain's Secret Alchemical Remedy for Victory and Fulfillment***) for an instantaneous transformation was performed with his twelve special disciples among the Knights Templar secret society of France which has not been revealed until this day. The reason for keeping the **GAM** secret was due to an extraordinary powerful in its essence. It is demonstrated in an unprecedented way which the usual ritualistic fashion was considerably elucidated. He eliminated most of the ceremonial implements, articles including majestic bestibes and ostentatious ceremonious orchestration. He kept only a torch, incense and simple white clothing with a cap: ankle length, kimono-style clothing made out of a linen type material for this **GAM**.

The secret **G**olden **A**lchemical **M**antra presented here in this book will easily be accepted and acquired by people of the current mode of lifestyle. This **GAM** has no correlation with a ritual of secret societies; the rituals of Initiation Rites of the secret societies in the past were usually conducted by the renowned adept and the members were limited to only prestigious personages, including Lords and Princes. These rituals were characterized by the elaborate usage of ceremonial orchestration, similar to the world's religious ceremonies that involve hours of preparation and majestic performances. These rituals were often conducted on certain days of the month, which were selected through astronomical patterns and complex mathematical calculations. Any Rites of Initiation rituals that St. Germain performed were also under the specific frame of astronomical predictions, which he often chose as the 5th, 15th, and 25th of the month. St. Germain's Secret Alchemical Remedy which contains the **G**olden **A**lchemical **M**antra in this book he practiced among his twelve disciples was on the 25th of each month for seven consecutive periods.

Nevertheless, this self-help book unveils St. Germain's secret Alchemical ingredient to live in miracles and his marvelous, prodigious wisdom; it is my duty to share his secret Alchemical treasure. It is profoundly associated with the nucleus of great wisdom of Divine: the richest fruition of Divine perennial wisdom intended to provide an instantaneous transmutation and grandeur transformation in your life. We realize that willpower itself is not enough to transcend the Self (internal) and the life (fulfillment of your dreams and desires). We need to acquire something extra. This book contains important ingredients necessary to create pursuance force; it conveys greater levels of advantage for anyone to experience miracle: Divine splendor of expansion and abundance. With grandeur transformation, it quickly reshapes your own reality at this time in life, after lifelong flounder through these mighty ingredients of the remedy and the marvelous wisdom.

Furthermore, this prodigious treasure can rapidly transcend your life into an alternate dimension of reality aiming to be who you really want to be, with the means of creating a new, constructively developed identity of your latent talents and abilities. Additionally, this secret Golden Alchemical Mantra possesses a greater potency for transmuting Karmic substance in the subconscious, with the intention of being free from misery and suffering due to deprivation and problems associated with the psycho/physical/emotional department.

We are all striving for permanent happiness and it is possible with the help of St. Germain's secret Golden Alchemical Mantra and perennial wisdom to create a life miracle. When you realize what this book can do for you, there is almost unlimited to what you can accomplish. It is said, in order to enter the Divine Kingdom of abundance, you must have a child-like heart. It opens your mind to a greater level of receptivity, and will increase your perception to undreamed futures.

Le Comte de St. Germain's colossal in heart, the secret Golden Alchemical Mantra has been emancipated to be accessible to humanity in this millennium. The time has come to rectify your life by way of infinite expansion to fulfill your destined and victorious path.

St. Germain states: **"This secret Golden Alchemical Mantra can bring you anything you desire in a substantial reality regardless of who you are or what your circumstances, as long as your desires are genuine with irrefutable conviction, which will be congenial to the Divine spirit. There is nothing you cannot do because you are an unlimited being and with the aid of my secret knowledge, you will be slide into a higher dimension, a domain of unlimited abundance, which is ready to provide you with anything that you ask for. You will experience the endless avenues of exploration and the dynamic self-transformation. Due to the secret power of its Hermetic essence, it causes three stages of chemical change: initiation, purification, and transformation. You may expect spontaneous constructive change in your internal and external life; eventually, you will go further than the problem of livelihood, and the mighty force is ready to transform the way of which you have dreamed. Due to this powerful alchemical essence, you will witness the impossible becoming possible, and justice coming out of injustice. You are now on the path of Divine miracle."**

It is possible with this book, *DIVINE AMBROSIA: HOW TO LIVE IN MIRACLES—St. Germain's Secret Golden Alchemical Mantra.*

# WHO IS LE COMTE DE ST. GERMAIN?

Although more than three hundred years have passed since his departure, he still exists. He is the eighteenth century's greatest European Alchemist, Le Comte de St. Germain, whose omnipresence is portrayed in texts, chronicles, and historical record. His remarkable achievements exemplified exceeding quality, which surpassed the normal view of human ability and genius; it was simply superlative and reflected on every field of scholarly, scientific, and diplomatic in the transcendental way. He was known to possess celestial powers and gave an impression of, "Anything he touches turns into gold." He was a man of intrinsic sophistication, great nobility, and gentility. He was truly an enlightened being.

During his revelation in life, he was called "He who does not die," remanifesting throughout the centuries, particularly in France, Italy, Scandinavia, Germany, and North America, to extol and exemplify freedom of consciousness; he willingly preserved the inherent, absolute right to experience life in accordance with our supreme conception of the Divine Spirit.

It has been proven that enlightened, historical personages such as Ezekiel the prophet, Lao, Tzu, Jesus Christ, Babaji, Mother Mary, St. Germain and others often emerged through the transfiguration of variable light: white, golden, purple, green, blue, pink, symbolized through hierarchy, characteristics, and qualities. Sometimes, it reveals more than its essence to an individual who has certain reincarnated connections.

# St. Germain's Noble Traits

St. Germain was born in August 15, 1704, the son of Prince Francis Ragoczy of Transylvania and his wife, Princess Takely. However, according to St. Germain, his biological mother was in fact, Princess Margareta, Princess Takely's youngest sister. Both Princesses were of the Medici dynasty. After Princess Takely's sudden death, Francis Ragoczy took a second wife. St. Germain was nine years of age at the time of her death.

Almost immediately after Prince Francis's new wife bore a son, St. Germain was separated from his father and officially adopted by the family of his biological mother. By this time, he was acknowledged as fine prodigy, exhibited extraordinary talents in everything he attempted; he mastered the eight different languages and the advanced levels of almost all the fields of academic knowledge. From the age of twelve through twenty-one, in Italy, he continued to extend his education aligned with the subject, which is more to do with Gnostic, esoteric, and occult. Italy was the center of the best education one could possibly obtain in that era. During those nine years of scholastic performance, St. Germain conceived the richest fruition and reached his greatest profundity. By age nineteen, he additionally acquired thirteen other languages.

Upon the completion of his education in Italy, he began traveling worldwide, tracing the footsteps of prototypes searching for an ancient knowledge and Divine perennial wisdom, aiming to acquire a supernatural power. St. Germain's primary interest was the Hermetic art: an accomplishment of the Philosopher's Stone: the passage of *prajna* to be among the chosen ones.

When he was 25 years of age, despite being heir to his father's throne, St. Germain wavered his rights but he was still entitled to be a part of most of his father's estates, assets, and various titles, in addition to his inheritances from his maternal side of the Medici dynasty. He established distinguished status and connection with people of the highest circles and has become known to be the celebrated being: the Greatest Alchemist and an adept, an initiator of rites, prevailed throughout Europe. His genius was in great demand and he frequently crossed the countries to fulfill his missions.

# St. Germain and King Louis XV

Diplomacy was St. Germain's primary mission. However, according to him, most of his diplomatic missions were often associated with King Louis XV's personal enquiries, which were to locate the neighboring kings' secret political affairs and their interests in the areas of development and expansion. Consequently, St. Germain became an important and unique personage with position and great influence on King Louis XV. His mission eventually evolved into a state of profound subject regarding issues of humanistic concerns that had not yet been revealed during his lifetime.

In exchange for conducting the King's private missions, St. Germain was offered prestige and status, and private residences in many regions, including an apartment in the French Courts: however, most of his work, including significant documents had been banished and destroyed by arson during the French Revolution.

On one occasion, St. Germain led me to retrace his footsteps in France, directing me on a path to locate his residence and the places where he often stayed during his lifetime. There is only one location visible, where evidence remains on public display at this time pertaining to the French government. In Le Chateau de Chambord, one can still observe the traces of his influence; St. Germain's apartment, which is located on the second floor of the north vestibule is aligned with the center portion of the main façade close to the apartment of the King. St. Germain's well-known portrait is framed on the wall near the door of his apartment. It reads, "Celebrated Alchemist," and explains, "This apartment was offered by King Louis XV."

# The Hermetic Revival

The Hermetic revival of the Renaissance was due to the rediscovery of the corpus *Hermetica*, which is believed to be an intrinsically ancient document. Thereafter, the Alchemy of the Italian Renaissance began constructing upon the ideas they embraced, and the foundations of modern chemistry were laid. It had accompanied a profound paradigm shift in the Renaissance worldview as though, had the eruption of Gnostic, Neoplatonic, and Hermetic writings in the early Christian period. These contemporary occurrences suggest that Alchemy is a perpetual subject and that it reflects the mind of its time. When the cultural imagination was greatly at work, transforming an old model into a new one, the fascination of Alchemy was intensified and its creative powers contributed to the changes that took place. In consequence, the highly sophisticated, considerable volume of manuscripts and the ancient secret texts of Divine Knowledge emerged.

This was the particular era in which St. Germain lived. It was an era of political confusion and it inspired many altruists to investigate the wisdom of the Esoteric, Gnostic science. St. Germain joined a Rosicrucian society at the age of 21; eight years later, he attained the Magnum Opus and his destiny became to usher his magnificent personality into the world.

# St. Germain and his Secret Manuscripts

According to St. Germain, he has written eight manuscripts of Initiation Rites. Most of his manuscripts are transcendental in nature; they contain the secret process by which the regeneration of humanity was to be accomplished and they also served as the key to his other writings and various missions. Essentially his work is derived from Gnostic, Esoteric, Occult, and Mystic, which are profoundly associated with Arabic, an ancient mystical Cabbalah, and the secret science of Egyptian (Alexandrian) Hermetic Art known as Alchemical Science.

The secret traditions of Initiation Rites were often conducted through complex writings and the symbolic representation of the universal knowledge. His work contains Divine Pymander, which involves the seventeen fragmentary writings that are integrated into the diverse secret ciphers of the enigmatic codes, the magical symbols, hieroglyphic figures, and various forms of ancient languages. The letters are written not only upside down and reversed in a back ward manner; they are written in certain alphabets and numbers are omitted or replaced by the various secret codes, symbols and unusual markings intend to conceal the great universal knowledge from the unworthy. But the secrets of the Divine power of the universe are given to those acquainted with their use of unlimited power over the spirits of the air and the subterranean divinities.

The titles of his manuscripts are: *The Saint; Company of God; The Sacred Attribute; Mystery Unveiled; The Great Magi and Divine Pymander; Holy Science: Divine Magic; The Ring of the Fire; The Saint, Magi and Seers; The Most Holy Wisdom.* These manuscripts were the nucleus of the various secret societies and were widely used among those organizations of Europe during and after his life. Two of the manuscripts surfaced in the public, yet they slipped away from the hands of the secret societies during the time of discontent in France.

# St. Germain & Alchemy

Originally, Alchemy was understood as an essentially symbolic language for spiritual realities and the ultimate symbolic representation of the transformation; it was illuminated as the transformation of tenebrous, leaden physicality of earthbound consciousness into the refined gold of a spiritually illuminated being who is doubtlessly concerned with inner dynamics resulting in the purification of the body, mind, and soul. Thus, St. Germain's true purpose and intention of his Alchemical Remedy is the transformation of the self by Divine initiation into the establishment of the noble ideas, aiming for its totality.

The Alchemical tradition is as old as the shaman, hermit, priesthood, and those pagan ritualistic lines and various Alchemical works and legacies that have been found throughout the world. However, the context of St. Germain's Secret Alchemical Remedy which was revealed in my book, ***Great Alchemist and Quantum Manifestation Power: St. Germain's Secret Alchemical Remedy*** is thought to be closely associated with Daoistic-Alchemy, Tantric-Alchemy, and mystic-Cabbala.

The ancient Alchemists were originally Hermits who resided in the mountain areas and who developed the methods of meditation and healing that provided insights leading to soul chemistry. Various spiritual and chemical experiments were later incorporated into traditional medicine and an original form of Oriental medicine was born. The esoteric side of alchemical virtue and practices is like preserving the essence of life's vital energy, which contributes to good health and longevity. For the Alchemists, gathering virtue is equivalent to gathering healing, and doing so maintained a long life. In order to stay in touch with our vital reserves with our inner strength, we do not waste life's energy or the vital essence. The basic principle of the key element is to attain by controlling, joining, and blending the body's own vital elements and forces. The preservation of life energy is similar to the practice of the Hindu yogi of "no action" (maintain one's center core to the main purpose only and drop the rest as unnecessary). The principle was to maintain the physical as well as the mental balance and harmony, inner unity and centeredness by living a life of moderation.

Traditionally, Alchemists practiced daily invocation and recitation of the Golden Alchemical Mantra. A practice containing recitation of the seventy-two Divine names, talismanic magic, herbal concoction, and meditative trance dance to awaken the psycho/physical essence and the supernatural power for transformation. Since Purple Light represents divinity, spirituality, healing power and Divine protection; thus, an invocation of the Purple Light to invite the medicine of healing was an essential part of their life.

Another important color and substance used in the Alchemist meditation and ritual was gold; it was an Alchemical symbol and an essential ingredient of Alchemy. The color gold is sacred, due to its purity and majesty. It represents power, longevity, prosperity, and transformation of the soul. It is symbolically interpreted as the untarnished pure state of being, wisdom, understanding, the pearl of enlightenment, and a source of Light. Thus, gold and purple are illuminated by flames to become the symbolic interpretation of wisdom. Alchemists throughout the ages believed that the essence of gold is the link between heaven and earth, and associated it with great work. The final stage of the Alchemical process, known as the Philosopher's Stone, is to be enlightened. It is said to be concealed in the formula **V.I.T.R.I.O.L.** (Visit the interior of the earth; through purification thou wilt find the hidden stone).

Alchemical writers were unanimous in preaching and promising the spiritual rewards of the art striving to protect Divine Science and sacred Alchemy from the misuse of power. As it is told in various myths and folklore, the primordial Gods hid the great power of the universe within the hearts of men to conceal its power.

# $P$ART II

# THE PANDORA'S BOX:

## THE DIVINE LAWS AND PERENNIAL WISDOM FOR AN INSTANTANEOUS TRANSFORMATION

*The Fear of the Lord is the Beginning*
*of Knowledge;*
*But Fools Despise Wisdom and Instruction.*

*Proverbs 1:7*

# THE PANDORA'S BOX

St. Paul explains the "inner experience" by which we come to know wisdom. He says, ***"We speak of wisdom among the perfect, not the wisdom of this world, nor of the rulers of this world, but divine wisdom in a mystery, secret, which none of the Archons of this world know."*** An initiation is an expansion of consciousness toward recognition of universal realities. The adepts, those who had received the keys, activated the wisdom that had been locked within the parable to construct their inherent, divine potential.

# THE PANDORA'S BOX 1
## The Divine Blueprint: The Secret Door of Your Destiny

One precept of Taoist doctrinereveals: **"There is or can be a winner inside: leaders, thinkers, or artists; there are dreams and desires, and needs. We are that being, uniquely called to occupy a precise place in the cosmic order no matter where or in what era we live. Everyone possesses that potential within; it can be reached within that particular being and manifested in the outer world."**

Mystics of all teachings suggest that each one of us has reincarnated into this life with a new purpose; perhaps one may have already been chosen for a path to pursue and the whole arrangement has been done in the manner of a Divine contract within the transitional world. It may be symbolically marked in one's DNA blueprint.

This is something so definite, something that cannot be ignored, as though the craving of the soul will one day demand its right to be fulfilled. Running away, escaping from the fulfillment of a destined path, might eventually cause one's normal function of the mind to lose orientation in life. As a result, one may not be here too long; he or she will be drawn back into the transition, or remain in this life with the feeling of floundering, homelessness, or having collective psycho/physical problems, including the self-destruction, which can occur. Perhaps the refusal of the core is more to do with one's karmic issues (karmic debt) that follows everywhere, even to the next reincarnation.

The refusal of the sermon baptizes the adventure into its negative world of apathy and melancholy. The subject isolating the power of the significant affirmative action becomes the victim to be saved. The refusal of the quintessence is essentially the refusal of the Self; it is to give up what it takes to fulfill one's own advantage. One's floundering world becomes the wasteland of the deterioration and decay, and the life existence becomes meaningless.

Plato explains that the Divine Design is a perfect geometric pattern, inviolable, indestructible, and inescapable in its essence. This is the perpetual, unchanging Divine Law of immaculate concept, which one has no choice but to fulfill in this life or the next. The super-conscious awareness of the puzzle pieces of life are representations of one's Divine Plan that the conscious mind often cannot see.

This is a Divine game and one must play with all the pieces of the puzzle to produce a perfect picture; one's destined blueprint guarantees victory and fulfillment at the time of completion as something too good to be true. This is the royal road surrounded by much Divine protection and intervention. Many helpers appear to advance the unmistakable Divine

Plan; it will never be with a sense of striving but rather frolic. In John (15:1-2), **"I am the true vine, and my Father is the vine-grower. He removes every branch in me that bears no fruit. Every branch that bears fruit he prunes to make it bear more fruit."** The Supreme Intelligence will remove those people out of your life who are not fruitful. Those who are fruitful, he will prune so they will bear more fruit. Pruning means, to some extent, bringing disciplines to help us trust the Supreme power of the universe; you will then cease desiring the wrong things, and the right desires will take their place.

When you have made this command, followed by great changes, a shift in life occurs, aiming to be transformed; it is a wondrous transition which you have to endure in order to come to the crossroad (mid-point) for the heroic venture. It is far from what you thought was your destiny, as though repulsive experience. However, re-adjustments will be done quickly for a new and wonderful wave of life.

Recite the **G**olden **A**lchemical **M**antra daily to magnify its power.

> **"I am the Divine Way,**
> **I am the Divine Truth,**
> **I am the Divine Life!"**

> **"I am the Divine Wisdom,**
> **All-Knowing Expression of Being!"**

Wise sages throughout the ages have said, **"Follow intuition, luck will incarnates naturally."** Since intuition is the Divine's unmistakable guidance, it is the greatest gift for all humanity; it is the nucleus of our being. Let Divine Intelligence arrange instead of arranging by logic.

Many things in life cannot be determined or defined by logic or reasoning especially when it comes to difficult decision-making. To see your Divine Kingdom in the quantum way requires a few specific conditions. Once you accept the destined path to follow, you must stay focused until you reach the destination. The sacred legacy warns, **"Do not turn back,"** or **"Do not turn to the right or to the left."** It also specifically suggests keeping silent on your intention, **"Tell no one,"** refraining from invective speech, sardonic remarks and any means of stigmatizing others in order to avoid attracting a similar energy to yourself. It is also important to keep human affiliation as minimal as possible to conserve the Divine power within.

According to the scripture, **"Anyone who hears my words and obeys them is like a wise man who reaches the high ground. But anyone who hears them and does not obey them is like a foolish man who forever stumbles ending in regret and sorrow."** It implies that one who consciously unites with the Cosmic invincible, experiences much blessing. Since we are under the Law of micro/macro cosmic structure as though we are mother and new-born babe connected with the umbilical cord, we can do the grandeur and substantial tasks if we are willing to work adjacent to the supreme energy, to be nurtured by its essence. The way of the wise is to trust and surrender rather than to navigating with logic, searching for a fantasy island or following someone else's idea. Parents' or one's father's path will likely prove to be unsuccessful or even disastrous in the end.

The Taoistic doctrine depicts, **"There are warriors, kings or sages in myself, to be a warrior in the outer world, one must be a warrior in the inner world; to be a king in the outer world, one must be a king in the inner world; to be a sage in the outer world, one must be a sage in the inner world."** The wise way of "nonresistance" is the supreme concept and energy, the key to a quantum jump. The scripture states your personal mind should act as a bystander, watching and praising the wisdom coming down through your super-conscious. Zero conflict within will, naturally and significantly, conserves the Divine power to the greatest degree for a greater cause. Therefore, surrender and drop the weapons to be free from unnecessary battle. Recite daily:

> **"I am the Divine Light and Reflection,**
> **I am the Divine Essence and Radiance!"**

> **"I am the Divine Conscious,**
> **I am the Divine Subconscious,**

## I am the Divine Super-conscious,
## The Manifest Perfection of Being!"

Myths and folklore explain a hero's journey as a customary hero on a destined path, being single hearted, mentally focused, and full of faith. What he finds will liberate him from his old identity, in a grand transformation, into an identity of full potential. A hero who remains on the heroic path will find God, and enter into the Divine Kingdom of unlimited abundance.

The hero, if successful in the adventure after the symbolic death and rebirth, returns to the cross road (the mid-point) where his journey began. This represents his psychological triumphs. In any victory, a person must be victorious in his or her mind after a symbolic death and rebirth. Even when a legend has a genuine historical personage, action and victory are demonstrated not in life-like, but in dream-like configurations. Finally, one's resistance has been conquered and the forgotten powers have revivified for the transfiguration of the world. When this deed is accomplished, life no longer suffers hopelessly under terrible disaster.

Finding your unique, inherent Divine-blueprint may not be an easy task to perform. Perhaps it is comparable to solving a puzzle whose destined path is hard to overtake. When you are sensitive to the sphere of energy, the conscious mind is receptive to intuitive guidance. Thus, guidance fills the mind with valuable information through perceptions as to what to do in life and when to do it. If you neglect to listen to the whisper within, or to the inner cry of the soul, you will miss what is trying to be revealed; it is your destined path that is hidden in the Pandora's Box. In order to reach that treasure, you must turn into the center of being to be led by reason. The mythic heroes will guide the one who accepts the hero's journey, the Divine soul.__

If you are on the destined path, you instinctively know that you are on the Royal Road of Guaranteed Path, and it is filled with divine aspirations to accomplish your task each day. With that, there is no sense of void or uselessness in the mind but there is happiness and contentment. You know that there is a divine energy working side by side with you to protect you from any destructive influences. Duties and affairs are smooth and harmonious in the face of your quick coming of accomplishment. Due to your captivating pursuit, the core self will never be anxious to flee from a day's work, and no longer envies anyone. It is said that the Divine Bluebird whispers into your ear if you are willing to listen. Therefore, if you are not on the right path of Divine-Blueprint, your experience is the opposite from the preceding statement. Obviously you are not living a life where true goals are active. It may not be fruitful in the end.

# THE PANDORA'S BOX 2
## The Secret Door of Power & Success

It has been told and understood that every human being possesses a remarkable innate quality. By identifying that something extra within, the mind has a clear focus for clustering and coalescing in your consciousness in order to work more constructively. That extra something within is your essence of Divine power which will expunge the shadows of self-scepticism and restore surety, bringing courage and ideas into action.

Mystics of all ages tell us that God's gift to man is an inherent, universal power (unlimited potential); the power to create or destroy lies within ourselves. However, you must know how to access that power which has been locked within the Pandora's Box (soul). Taoist doctrine depicts that the secret of true power is "fearlessness," "nonresistance" and the belief that **"One who is fearless is crowned."**

It must be true that, "All unhappiness comes from lack of power." Many people invest themselves in constructing their dream house on sand through constant expenditure of psycho/physical energy in human affairs; there will be nothing left but the enshrinement of one's highest potential. This is precisely depicted in the Eastern doctrine of, "A few words are silver, but silence is gold." The more you merge with the Divine essence, the more you transcend into becoming an unlimited being. It has been stated in the ancient texts, "What is above is what is below." The scripture assures, "We are the mirror image with Supreme Intelligence." We are within the micro/macro cosmic frame and order. This direct relation signifies that there is no division between heaven and earth; the statement of "Supreme Intelligence and I are one;" the micro and macro-cosmos are within ourselves. What is above equals what is below; therefore, the human being can express the same power in the outer world. Great men throughout the ages have proven to be true that they have accomplished seemingly impossible superhuman, transcendental tasks.

**"One will be blessed and receive the gift who asks, or find the truth who seeks."** What you desire immediately reflects into the imperceptible mirror; all the good that is to be made manifest in man's life is previously manifested fact in the Divine plan. Therefore, let Supreme Intelligence know your desires, invite that unlimited source of abundant supply, and be fulfilled. The scripture suggests, wherever it has done miracle before for others, the miracle will be done for you too. Realizing this truth and following the Divine guide, your every need will be taken care of now and forever more. With the help of St. Germain's **G**olden **A**lchemical **M**antra, you can now draw an unlimited supply through the Divine fountain of abundance with constant expectancy, and you can now begin to release the dynamic phase of Divine superpower.

> **"I am the Divine Essence and Magnificence,
> I am the Divine Victory and Fulfillment!"**

> **"I am the Divine Power and Essence,
> I am the Divine Perfection and Manifestation!"**

Recite this daily in preparation for full readiness in enforcing your inner power of Divine essence with the intention of maximizing the effect of its power. In the means of, **"Be ye transformed yourself by renewing of your mind,"** this will help to transmute the negative stigma in the subconscious that is impeding your path into the powerful, immediate Divine influence. Expand your awareness of the breadth of your body, from the top of your head, to the bottom of your toes, and you will soon transform to be powerful, energetic, confident, and knowing how to live every facet of your life.

# How to Determine Your Destined Goal

To win your victory and fulfillment in life, certain goals must be established.  Without goals, there is no sense of objective, and the psychic energy tends to ramble and become distracted from accomplishing anything in life.  This expends your valuable energy worthlessly; therefore, you come to the point where life is inconsequential and discontent.  Many things in life, unhappiness arises from not fulfilling your goals. Conversely, in order to be happy, you must accomplish the goal(s). Goals (inherent purpose), therefore, are indispensable parts of human life.

Since the world can offer various opportunities and endless material supplies, it is not easy choice to determine which one of your goals will bring you substantial success.  Often your true goal (mission in life) is still hidden in the subconscious, locked and waiting to be recognized.

One way to determine your true goal is by listing all of your possible goals (desires); list what you wish to accomplish in order of importance. Reevaluate the list, examine why, what is the motive behind each goal, and find what you are still drawn to.  This is an excellent strategy for those who are uncertain and who face utterly blind future courses of action.  The best, however unbeatable way to determine your true goal is to recite the **GAM** to call on the Supreme Energy and receive guidance. The answer will surface in a blink of an eye.

> **"I am the Divine Designed life,**
> **I am the Divine Designed Path,**
> **I am the Divine Destiny**
> **And Manifest Perfection of Being!"**

You may think you want something, only to realize afterwards that it may not be in your best interest. In most cases, the accomplishment comes when you are fully ready to receive with no fear. Once again, **"One who is fearless is absolute."** There are no further conflicts between the conscious and subconscious mind. Thus, the intuition "super-conscious idea," a perfect "Divine" idea, can easily enter in your mind. Recite daily to awaken the Divine power within:

> **"I am the Divine Power and Order,**
> **I am the Divine Action and**
> **Manifestation!"**

Accomplishing your goals requires a consistent attitude toward ultimate completion. The adverse thoughts of self-scepticism and worry are the corruptors of your righteous desires, which are easily distorted by listening and granting; they soon become monstrous and rebellious. Thus, it is vital to dissolve any thoughts that are blocking your success and achievements. Fear is especially fatal; it can jeopardize your intention, and total failure can occur. It is as though fear is twisting your destiny into broken form. The best way to maneuver out of this negative condition is to establish unconquerable affirmative consciousness within. Recite the **GAM** daily; call on the Supreme Intelligence for guidance, for the exact course of action and direction. If your goal is within the Divine loop, success is guaranteed in which the daily work will be enthusiastic, and effortless; you reach the destination in the quantum way. Thus, now is the time to act towards your desired goal in a productive way.

# The Key to Unfolding the Universal Divine Energy

It is an obvious fact that all human accomplishments require an expenditure of energy, and the laws controlling that supply of energy must be expended wisely. The Law of Like Attracts Like demonstrates that every thought is examined as a psychic functional energy and has a captivating quality; it makes contact with everything in our psycho/physical conditions and affairs. It implies that positive circumstances are conceived by positive attitude, in that an invocation to the universe draws to you the resemblance of your thoughts, which results in successful interactions. Each of different wavelengths of the psychic energy corresponds to the Like emotion in people's lives. Thus, distracting thoughts, words, and deeds telepathically repel and reap distracting results. Likewise, if you seek love, prosperity, and success, the mind will attract and broadcast them accordingly. You are literally drawing them to yourself through your psychic energy. In other words, you should be careful about what you ask for, and it is required for maintaining an affirmative mental attitude to bring about a decisive way of life.

Furthermore, when practicing the principal of victory and fulfillment, you should persist with the attitude that you are consistently collaborating with the Laws of Energy. In order to achieve success, you must have a solid idea of success. The scripture warns, **"Turn not from it to the right nor to the left, that thou mayest have good success whithersoever thou goes."** If you follow the admonition, you will be on the throne with the crown of righteousness. It also warns that your intention shall not depart from the mouth, but, "Thou shalt meditate therein day and night, that thou mayest observe to do all that is written therein, for then wilt thou make thy way prosperous and thou shalt have good success." Adjacent to this principle, practicing silence will further intensify the Divine power within. Silence has been practiced by mystics of all ages; it protects your desired goals from interference. It maintains purity in your soul; therefore, let it expand on the inner horizon.

# How to Void Negative Traits and Dark Emotions

Negative thoughts incessantly slither into our consciousness and beat the manifestation of our heart's desires. The more you discern negative thoughts, the more you ratify it and eventually becomes brutal; however, affirmative thoughts are just as systematic as negative thoughts. Destructive attitudes become predominant because we do not properly emphasize our constructive beliefs; this concept has well been defined by the Buddhist doctrine of release. An intense condition prevails when you nourish it with your own intensity. If we withdraw this intensity, the problem loses its vitality itself. Often mystify and instigate patterns are solved by releasing them with harmonious thoughts, rather than by any elaborate justification. As soon as you release problems, peace of mind will be restored and the problems can no longer impel or injure the person. When this concept has been installed, new dimensions will arise with a brand new worldview.

The scripture states, **"Out of the imaginations of the heart come the issues of life."** Thus, never embrace the idea of lack or deprivation, or the rigid idea of life being hard and filled with disappointments. Also persevere against painful memories of hatred, because resentment will poison the psycho/physical department and affairs. When energy is constantly reflected back, it is like a psychic relapse or possession with past events, while good opportunities pass by and you lose the chance to expand and grow in the particular moment in life. Living in the past, lamenting your misfortunes, talkativeness, and gossip scatter your Divine power within. The influence of others in one's earlier years helped to convey negative traits, which have been inhibiting and repressing one's full potential from gaining the best that life has to offer. Now is the time to see through sickness into health, to see through limitation into abundance.

Recite the **GAM** daily--bring heaven on earth--to restore the years of good, eaten by locusts. With the powerful effect of its essence, you will be amazed how fast your adverse ideas are replaced with Divine power and ideas of success.

> **"I am the Divine Conscious,
> I am the Divine Subconscious,
> I am the Divine Super-conscious!"**

> **"I am the Divine Law and Order,
> I am the Divine Justice and Grace!"**

> **"I am the Divine Life,
> I am the Divine Future,
> I am the Divine Victory and
> Fulfillment!"**

Others will soon realize that you are a new person with a new way of leading your life.

# THE PANDORA'S BOX 3

## Three Divine Secret Powers:

The Power of Intuition
The Power of Prayer
The Power of Faith

## THE DIVINE SECRET 1

## The Power of Intuition "Supreme Knowing"

Through intuition we know that there is an inherent genius within, locked, but that can be captured by the cultivation of receptivity; thus, **"Awake thou that sleepeth."** To follow intuition is to follow Divine guidance (enlightened, the state of super-profitability), which is the greatest discovery of humanity. The leaders of the world excelled their abilities through their intuitive guidance to become the greatest leaders. Intuition assists us to reach the truth of any matter quickly. Da Vinci states, "All our knowledge has its origin in our perceptions" which is the key to opening the doors to the Divine Kingdom of unlimited abundance. Divine wisdom rushes through perceptions: a flash of vision, inspiration, a hunch or sound, persistence in getting attention, pointing the way to where the treasures are hidden. The Divine Way of revealing the path to the treasure is playful and can be quite tricky; apparently, insignificant events can be a trigger to the crux of the matter or to the definite path to one's goal. In other words, it can be an exit from the labyrinthine confusion into an instantaneous discovery of the treasure.

Many secrets are revealed through the senses, especially vision as a powerful and Divine instrument to convey your desires into physical reality. Knowing how to see is the foundation of All-knowing. The Taoistic point of view explains, **"When man loses his sight, he loses his view of the universe"**; the eye is truly the window of the soul. King Solomon was considered a man of great wisdom and understanding because he dared to follow his intuition. As he promised, the man who dares to follow his intuitive understanding will have a long life, riches, honor, health and happiness (Proverbs 3). The statement **"Acknowledge me in all your ways and I will make a plan in your path"** is the truth.

Nearly everyone has, at some point in life, tasted this secret wisdom as inherent, spontaneous knowing, and has been astonished at its revelations, believing in the saying, **"Trust in me, commit your ways unto me."** The various sacred scriptures explain that in order to enter the wondrous land of infinite possibility, you must possess the heart of a little child. Follow the intuition of the unmistakable, royal road, the golden harvest is automatic!

# Follow the Path of Divine Miracle

The Taoistic point of view of Nonresistance is expressed in, **"Don't choose but follow intuition."** Intuition is a spontaneous natural wisdom, an effortless and precise path of Divine Order. One who only follows the path of Aristotelian may find it difficult to follow intuition; presumably they do not trust intuitive answers. It seems that intuition and logic are not exactly on friendly terms; intuitive guidance often shuts off as soon as logic intervenes, almost as though oil and water. All the painful lessons that come through blundering ignorance, through making wrong decisions, or going the wrong direction, can be avoided by connecting with the Supreme Intelligence, so that you are under the Divine influence of protection and assistance. The path of wisdom certainly gives you a splendid advantage.

# THE DIVINE SECRET 2
# The Power of Prayer: The Sacred Dialogue with Divine

Prayer is indispensable to the work of Alchemy and this characteristic distinguishes Alchemy from purely physical science. The aim of Alchemy is always to solemnly enlighten in a spiritual sense, aiming for monumental transformation, a transcendentally Divine state of being. They lived by the principles of simplicity and solitude: observing the self and the natural world where the beauty of nature is transformed into a gold-like state of perfection, the gold of longevity, inner power of potential, the strength of character. They practiced humility, respect, generosity, and kindness, seeking inner truth instead of rigidly, following the rules of conduct. It is the divine totality, "absolute pure metal." These are the core Alchemist virtues. Thus, prayer is an integrating power and spiritual unification, an essential part of human life since it magnifies human purposes. Practicing combined prayer and Perennial Wisdom heightens the sensibility within, show us our place in the cosmos, and teaches us how to become explorers.

# Prayer: The Divine Sentiment

Prayer has become somewhat defunct; it has diminished into a lost art. Many of us are swallowed up by the current trend of affairs to the point where we cannot spare a minute to say hello to Divine Intelligence until the Judgment Day arrives. There is an old saying that God and the doctor are useful in time of trouble, and are forgotten when the trouble ends. Prayer is usually called upon when misfortune strikes, and subsides from our attention when the threat has passed. The need for spiritual unity is eternal; it should be integrated into daily life, instead of when, rarely, a critical or calamitous event occurs. Therefore, prayer itself is a preventive medicine. As Plutarch depicts, **"The hearts and souls of men still seek the Deity and desire the experience of the God."** Biographical sketches reveal that all great men throughout the ages have lived with prayer as their consecration to Supreme principles and have practiced prayer as a conventional pathway to a life of wisdom. It said that the secret wisdom lies within the depth of prayer and it is illustrated by Pythagoras as an "Infinite Being, whose body was composed of the substance of truth." Divinity is an eternal reason, an absolute intellect, manifesting through wisdom, love, and strength. The conventional concept, which is supported by great men in the world, prominently, Plato and Socrates, is that it is a natural instinct to pray to the universal Creator, or the primordial Gods, who have emanated from the original principle.

# Prayer as the Therapeutic Power

The 15<sup>th</sup> century greatest physician and Alchemist, Paracelsus, believed that various physical ailments begin with stress and anxiety, a result medically proven to be true. However, mystics of all ages explain that these adverse elements originate in resentment, fear, jealousy, and evil-intention of those dark emotions. He states that faith would cure all diseases. Faith is an inner conviction and sacred contract between micro/macro cosmos. It is a Divine matrix, a state of certainty, of super-assurance. Faith is a divine fountain of energy. Many nations still actively employ various methods of healing practices that include sacred Prayer, Mantras, and certain decrees to alleviate various elements in the body.

According to the Divine Law, almost all diseases are visualized in one's mind's eye first, before they are manifested in a physical reality, since the universal energy follows one's idea. Your consistent imagery becomes the crystallized reality. All the prayers in the world cannot heal or effectively support the idea of ill health as "necessary," or "unavoidable." Your faith (belief) has a manifesting power; it will always be manifesting on the things in which you hold unbroken faith.

# THE DIVINE SECRET 3
# The Power of Faith: The Divine Golden Matrix

When the human psyche unites with divine reflection, a chemical change occurs in the psycho/physical department; with faith, one stimulates the Divine healing power within and accelerates the transmutation process. In the act of unbreakable faith, even when the obstacles are most dire, circumstances will capitulate to the dynamic forces of the Divine Intelligence. The proverb of **"Follow the way of the wise"**: the smooth and joyful ride is assured, instead of navigating by trial and error in stormy weather forcing your personal will against the great force of the universe.

According to Paracelsus, sacred prayer, mantra, and decree are decisive and constructive statements of conviction, and naturally are associated with faith. Active faith is one of the great secret-substances for quantum manifestation. Active faith is a pursuance force that intensifies the passing process to reach the destination of your dreams and desires. In prayer with faith, the mind and emotions are stimulated with noble sentiments, and the realization that the Supreme intelligence is the great physician.

# How to Release the Divine Power

Various sacred tales illustrate, **"Even if an evil judge could be worn down by being asked over and over for help, God will also hear the prayers of his people who pray day and night."** It seems that God wants to hear your prayer/mantra (holy syllabus) over and over again. Alchemists throughout the ages often experienced miracles by reciting countless numbers of the Golden Alchemical Mantra(s) daily. It is said in the scripture, **"Ask and it shall be given to you."** This famous "plausible" statement is void by many people. The human psyche is programmed to believe that, "Life is hard....Nothing is easy,"

"Nothing should easily be obtained!"

According to the Divine Law, all the things for one asks in prayer shall be received. Many people have not employed the power of prayer due to misconception that it is wrong to pray for material things. The proverb of, "One who becomes the master of faith" also becomes the master in every aspect of life. One who prays (asks) with the attitude of nonresistance combined with conviction will be heard. **"Trust in me (faith) and I will bring it to pass."** Unbreakable faith, therefore, is the nucleus of manifestation process.

# PART III

# The Divine Solution

## GOLDEN BOUGH

*Knowledge is the Great Sun of the Firmament.*
*Life and Power are Scattered with All Its Beams.*

*Daniel Webster*

# The Golden

# Alchemical Mantra:
## The Divine Golden Ingredient

## Miracle Bringer

Mantras are powerful Divine verbal injections to the inner-mind. They are a dynamic way to restore Divine power in your conscious and subconscious mind to work more efficiently for you. Recite the **Golden Alchemical Mantra** daily, and you will suddenly have a vision of realization. More importantly, it magnifies the quantum manifestation power of Alchemical Programming. Due to the dynamic Alchemical transfusion, an instantaneous transmutation occurs while healing and purification are on the way to restore the Divine power, and you soon feel an archaic conditions stripping off, peace of mind being restored, and joy of heart reviving. The restrictiveness of the ancient tower of Babel is now torn down, breaking down negative thought patterns and dark emotions in the subconscious.

The **GAM** contains only the sacred and mighty Divine word. What you are engraving in the subconscious during the programming or reciting is only an affirmative, constructive, and transcendental Divine statement. It absolutely has no sense of negative connotation whatsoever. It is important not to mention words that connote negative emotions and vibrations: e.g. "My karma," "My dark emotions," "My old bad records," etc. that you are unintentionally engraving on the subconscious.

# Technique

Select the **G**olden **A**lchemical **M**antra that appeals to your heart the most and recite it over any situation. It is your golden bough and will perform miracles whenever you apply it. It is a Divine treatment, whenever you feel a real need to integrate your life with the supreme source of magnificent energy. The **GAM** should be said consciously, so that the meaning is infused in the subconscious memory bank of the mind. As the subconscious mind governs overall conscious decision-making, it can be a powerful instrument to maintain a positive and conscious attitude in controlling those rebellious emotions.

As you recite the **GAM** (s), visualize your desires in your hands! This is an essential key for a successful procedure, which means believing you already have accomplished the goal, and this is the Divine Way; therefore, the Divine Truth will manifest!

# INVOCATION FOR PROTECTION

"I Invoke the Purple Light of the Most High,
 Expanding Fire Breath of Divine Intelligence!"

"I am the Purple Light, I am the Expanding
 Fire Breath of Divine Intelligence!"

"Divine Protection,
 Divine Protection,
 Divine Protection!"

"Purple Light,
 Purple Light,
 Purple Light!"

# RIGHT PATH/GUIDANCE

"I am the Divine Life,
  I am the Divine Way,
  I am the Divine Truth,
  I am the Manifest Perfection of Being!"

"I am the Divine Wisdom,
  All-knowing Supreme Being!"

# POWER and SUCCESS

"I Knock Upon the Door of the Divine Kingdom
  Of Consciousness within me,
  Let it be Manifest now,
  Let it be Abundant now!"

"I am the Divine Law and Wisdom,
  I am the Divine All-knowing,
  Perfect Expression of Infinite Being!"

"I am the Divine Unlimited Being,
  I am the Divine Unlimited Potential,
  I am the Divine Creation and Manifestation!"

"I am the Divine Alpha and Omega,
  I am the Divine Omnipotence!"

"I am the Divine Power and Action,
  I am the Divine Charisma!"

"I am the Divine Essence,
  I am the Divine Radiance,
  I am the Divine Magnificence!"

"I am the Divine Life and Action,
  I Bear the Fruits of Divine Perfection!"

"I am the Divine Miracle,
  Manifest Perfection of Being!"

"I am the Divine Wisdom,
 I am the Divine Action and Speech!"

"I am the Divine Creator,
 I Co-create Victory
 And Fulfillment in my Life!"

"I am the Divine Splendor and Power,
 Miracle Manifests through me Everywhere!"

"I am the Divine Perfect Health,
 I am the Divine Perfect Wealth,
 I am the Divine Perfect Happiness,
 I am Victory and Fulfillment!"

"I am the Divine Power,
 I am the Divine Miracle,
 I am the Divine Charisma!"

"I am the Divine Demonstration,
 Completion and Perfection!"

# ETERNAL LOVE, BEAUTY, and LIFE

"I am the Divine Eternal Youth,
  I am the Divine Eternal Beauty,
  I am the Divine Eternal Life!"

"I am the Divine Life and Order,
  I am the Divine Love and Unity
  Perfect Expression of Being!"

"I am the Divine Love and Grace,
  I am the Divine Beauty and Youth
  Radiant Expression of Being!"

"I am the Divine Irresistible Magnet
  And Attraction;
  Illimitable Light of Being!"

"I am the Divine Peace and Harmony,
  I am the Divine Regeneration
  And Rejuvenation!"

"I am the Divine Eternal Life,
  I am the Divine Eternal Youth,
  I am the Divine Eternal Beauty
  Ageless, Deathless Expression of Being!"

"I am the Divine Love and Harmony,
  I am the Divine Illimitable Light and Healing,
  I am the Supreme Law of Divine Grace!"

# KARMIC HEALTH ISSUES:
## Recurring, Hereditary, Malignant Growth

"I am the Divine Law and Order,
 I am the Divine Grace and Harmony,
 I am the Divine Purification
 And Transformation!"

"I am Divine Intelligence,
 I am Divine Omnipotence,
 I am Divine Omniscience!"

"I am the Divine Resurrection,
 I am the Divine Ascension
 I am the Divine Transcendental Being!"

 "I am the Divine Essence
 And Transcendence!"
  I am the Light of the World!"

"I am the Divine Light and Illumination,
 I am the Divine Life and Reflection,
 Manifest Perfection of Being !"

"I am the Divine Essence,
 I am the Divine Body, Mind, and Soul!"

"I am the Divine Ever-Rejuvenating,
 Ever-Regenerating, Ever-Illuminating
 Expression of Divine Essence!"

# FORGIVENESS

"I am the Divine Law and Grace,
  I am the Divine Light and Healing,
  Forgiveness Everywhere!"

"I am the Divine Law and Grace,
  I am the Divine Unity and Harmony,
  Forgiveness Everywhere!"

# PROSPERITY

"I am the Divine Prosperity and Abundance,
 I am the Divine Perfection and Manifestation,
 I am the Victory and Fulfillment!"

"I am the Divine Abundance,
 I am the Divine Fulfillment,
 I am the Divine Manifest Perfection
 Of Being!"

"I am the Divine Abundance;
 Inexhaustible Resources and Supply!"

"I am the Divine Great Financial Resources
 And Independence!"

"I am the Divine Life and Plan,
 Unlimited Abundance!"

# HAPPINESS

"I am the Divine Life and Joy;
  Happiness Manifests through me
  Everywhere!"

"I am the Divine Love and Happiness
  Manifest Perfection of Being!"

"I am the Divine Love and Grace,
  Harmony and Unity,
  Manifests through me Everywhere!"

"I am the Divine Way,
  I am the Divine Truth,
  I am the Divine Life
  Manifest Perfection of Being!"

# APPRICAIONS

# THE GOLDEN ALCHEMICAL MANTRA
## (MIRACLE BRINGER)

### For:

- **Transcend Your Self and Your Life into Splendor of Divine Miracle: Expansion and Abundance!**
- **Accomplish Your Divine Designed Goal (Destined): The Best and the Perfect Self Expression to Fulfill Your Destiny!**
- **Transform Yourself to be Who You Want to be: Being Transformed into Divine Splendor of Mega, Dynamic Reality!**
- **Transmute Dark Emotions into Unconquerable, Affirmative, and Constructive Reality!**

- **Balance the Outstanding Karmic Substance to be Free from Misery, Lack and Limitation in Life!**

The **G**olden **A**lchemical **M**antra can bring
an instantaneous manifestation, which can take you
into the vigorous swing of the Divine pathway; what
you need to do is to pull the string and the rest is
automatic. You will realize how powerful this **GAM**
is and your ingrained desires will be quickly delivered
by the Divine rights, which everyone possesses. It
will help you to choose the desired seeds that are
unique, divinely oriented specific seeds that will
quickly sprout up into the golden harvest of the
Divine fountain. It will shorten the path between
your desire and goals significantly. It is as though the
geometric design of your life is now unfolding for the
grandiose experience.

The effect of powerful chemical change,
which is produced through **GAM**, will result in a
spontaneous transmutation which creates an vehement
pacifying action on the conscious and the deeper level
of the subconscious realm. Inevitably, it will bring
dramatic change in your internal and external life;
it is a symbolic rebirth (resurrection) into a new and
wonderful phase of life. As soon as you recite it, you
quickly come to the crossroads (mid-point) that will
separate an old limited condition of the soul from a
new state of unlimited expansion. It is said, practice
makes perfect; thus, reciting this **GAM** sharpens
your intuition and intensify the connection with the
universal macro-cosmic energy, and you will see the
manifestation of your righteous desires.

The Taoistic doctrine states, **"To be great
in the outer world, one must be great in the inner
world."** For this, one must consciously link with the

macro cosmic energy to charge the Divine command. The wise, throughout the ages, achieved this state by absolute surrender to the supreme energy; this is the Divine Law and it is the only way and many great accomplishments have been done with the Divine command. One who lives in that state of mind will prove that it is so. With the help of St. Germain's Secret Alchemical Remedy, you can expect that any seemingly impossible good can overtake in an amazing way. Just omit your reasoning; the Divine way is mysteriously perfect.

# How to Win The Game of Life

## The Key Factors for the Quantum Manifestation Power: How to Prepare (Exhilarate) for Receiving Your Desires

St. Germain's comment: **"The way of the wise is to ask Divine Design of your life which is already in your inherent Divine geometric pattern and will manifest your desires smoothly and effortlessly in the quantum way once this secret is revealed from within; you have to implant a new geometric pattern without predecessor that will often result in straggle with time consuming effort followed by a countless number of trials and errors."**

It is stated, **"According to your faith, be it unto you."** Acting at any moment and preparing for good is another key to exhilarate the Quantum Manifestation process. It is wise to protect your intention in the heart without telling anyone, **"Tell no one,"** the proverbs warn, **"The world belongs to the silent one!"** Be familiar with the process and continually recite the appropriate Golden Alchemical Mantra for your desires to come into the visible light.

Consciously fix your mind on the image of your desired object in the form of a motion picture conjoint with emotion. Pay attention to how you are feeling when submitting your query. (An imprecise question--unsure mind--invariably yields unclear results). It can induce the desired image further and accelerate the quantum manifestation process. Also it helps to place a photograph to indicate your goal, to get in the vibration. Your desires must be clear in your mind's eye, though; these desires are ingrained in your soul in predestined manner.

Another key to accelerate the process is to salute the Divinity within with an attitude of rejoicing and expressing gratitude to the Divine Intelligence; it is a means of uniting, engaging with the Supreme Energy. A strong connection easily attracts and draws that energy toward yourself and your desires. It is said, **"Before ye call I shall answer."** Also, **"It is your Father's good pleasure to give you these things."** Realize this truth by knowing that manifesting your desires (goals) is a consequence of your attunement with the Divine mind within.

Therefore, by reciting the **G**olden **A**lchemical **M**antra(s) daily will opens all of your channels and the flow of energy from the Divine Spirit that will carry out your desires into a tangible reality.

# **T**echnique:

Before you apply this program, believe in the truth that your mind is a mental magnet; it can draw victory and fulfillment in your life. Surrender and trust, leave it in the hands of Divine energy. Link to the supreme, the rest is smooth and automatic on the Divine path.

Recite **GAM** daily, breathe through your entire being with the Golden liquid of Alchemical Mantra(s), and try to visualize that feeling of drinking it into your body. Do this by continually allowing only good and prosperous thinking to be engaged in your mind. Such thoughts are as seeds; they take root in the fertile soil of your mind, grow, and spread their roots and effects into the mind of Supreme Intelligence.

At the end of the **GAM**, it is necessary to seal the Divine contract by stating, **"So be it"** to enforce the power. This is the way the energy is sealed from any interference; it is the golden rule of Alchemical contract to achieve manifestation. This process can be done whenever you feel a real need to synthesize your life with a universal divine resource.

# Preparation

Prepare your heart's desires—bring an image of your true longing, which already been expanded within your heart for a certain period of time. It is something that you cannot ignore, something that has been ingrained in your soul. **Throughout the recitation of the GAM, keep focusing on the attention of the 7th chakra** (at the crown of your head). As soon as you become accustomed to it, you begin to feel a very gentle electric current of magnetic energy throughout your body.

# Procedure

First relax, become quiet for a moment. When you are ready, invoke the most high, a powerful protection of Divine source: **Purple Light.**

> **"I invoke the Purple Light**
> **Of the Most High,**
> **Expanding Fire Breath**
> **Of Divine Intelligence!"**

The next, register your heart's desire in your mind's eye. Gradually enter into a state of psychic wholeness and bring your desired thoughts ready to connect to your desired object (coalesce around that pattern with the Divine Golden Light, the essence of abundance). When you are done, recite the following **GAM**. Now is the time to change your self-image into what you wish to be.

**"I now Knock Upon the Door**
**Of the Divine Kingdom**
**Of Unlimited abundance within me,**
**Let it be Manifest now,**
**Let it be Manifest now!"**

**"I am the Divine Unlimited Being,**
**I am the Divine Unlimited Potential,**
**I am the Divine Unlimited Creation**
**And Manifestation!"**

**"I am the Divine Prosperity**
**And Abundance,**
**I am the Divine Perfection**
**And Manifestation,**
**I am the Divine Victory**
**And Fulfillment!"**

Anyone can have a quantum manifestation instantaneously, if you are truly ready!  The higher you go (by increasing your vibration to a new level of expectancy) the more rapidly your desires will manifest into reality.

# GAM FOR THE RIGHT PATH:
## Divine Designed Life for the Destined Goal

Not everyone found the true goals or even one knows what the righteous heart's desires, and often pursue goals that are far from Divine Plan. To find one's destined goal is to recite the following **GAM** continually. The answer will soon be delivered. Integrate into visualization.

> **"I am the Divine Way,**
> **I am the Divine Truth,**
> **I am the Divine Life**
> **I am the Completion and**
> **Perfection!"**

# GAM FOR POWER AND SUCCESS

Negative thoughts easily creep in, often jeopardizing your highest potentials (the Divine Rights) and the good that comes with it. It seems the more you reject them mentally trying to eliminate them, the more they rebound with multiple forces. If you are convinced that you are a failure, the Divine Law of Like Attracts Like will soon prove it to be true. Universal energy constantly responds to your thoughts and beliefs. If you ask for success and prepare for success, you will receive what you ask for. However, if you are convinced that you will not succeed, your contradiction of words and deeds will disrupt the Divine energy; consequently, it can result in failure. The Taoistic doctrine depicts, **"To be a leader in the outer world, one must be a leader in the inner world."** Thus, if you desire a wonderful life, you must have wonderful ideas and an attitude about life to be manifested in the outer world.

Self-doubt and fear are your biggest obstacles. They prevent you from advancing towards success and hold you back from taking important actions. These emotions often bury your highest potentials, jeopardize your perfect self-expression entirely. Self-doubt creates confusion in every aspect of life, for it confuses the entire Alchemical programming. Faith and full conviction are the key factors for bringing your desires into tangible reality. With the help of St. Germain's secret **G**olden **A**lchemical **M**antra, you will overcome your ingrained fear in the subconscious and restore the Divine Power within. When it is restored, you are on the way to the path of grand transformation. It is said, "One who is fearless, he is absolute," there is nothing that cannot be done. Throw away your old contract of the Hangman's Life that restricts and paralyze your life. Recite the **GAM** (s) daily and transmute those distractive emotions of fear and self-doubt. This will accelerates Dissolution of Karma Remedy and this will further trenchant into the subconscious realm and renewing your mind. One's subconscious must be brighter than the sun to see miracle everyday. Integrate into visualization.

> **"I am the Divine Way,**
> **I am the Divine Truth,**
> **I am the Divine Life,**
> **I am the Divine Illimitable Light**
> **and Essence,**
> **Manifest Perfection of Being!"**

You will soon find the appearance of obstacles quickly evaporating into thin air and all that you desire or require will be yours. Once you fully connect with the Divine energy, the response is instantaneous. Be alert and awake to good! It is said, **"In order to enter into the Divine Kingdom of abundance, you must keep the child at heart."** Be joyous, enthusiastic and filled with the expectancy for what you are receiving in any moment.

# GAM for an Immediate Supply

There is nothing wrong with being rich; in fact, money itself is good and beneficial. Without money, life is inconvenient. The only thing that creates misery in life associated with money is when you follow the path of selfishness, greed, or destructive purposes; inconsequence, your universal supply eventually vanishes. It is said in the scripture, **"One who ignores the Divine Law brings about his own destruction."** Following the Law of Consequences, "if you denounce money, you will be denounced by money. It will not attract the Divine supply or even if you do, will be only temporary. Perhaps the biggest pitfall for people who lack money is detaching themselves from the prosperity consciousness. It is common that people of certain genre of professions and religious fanatics often keep an automatic perception in the back of their head, constantly reminding themselves that "Love of money is the root of all evil." Your contempt for money separates you from money and hinders you from being prosperous. The Taoistic doctrine clarifies its essence, **"To be prosperous in the outer world, you must be prosperous in the inner world."** The phenomenal nature of the world and tangible world are interchangeable; it cannot stand alone, it must be integrated into one another or eventually prove it to be a short circuit.

The belief of old religious doctrines and convictions that money equals impurity, cause of all evil, must be changed to receptive attitude or you will be robbed of luck in money.  Recite the **GAM** (s) daily for an instantaneous transmutation, healing, and to be fully ready to be prosperous.  Integrate into visualization.

> **"I am the Divine Unlimited Abundance,**
> **I am the Divine Great Financial Resources**
> **And Independence!"**

The simple fact is that a man of wealth has a fixed idea on wealth, and conversely, the poor man, of poverty.  If you are sensitive to the universal energy, you instinctively acknowledge that the Supreme Intelligence is your only true source of supply.  Surrender and trust to the magnificent, abundant energy; it will soon bring you miracles.

# Alchemical Golden Light Prayer for Abundant Prosperity

"Golden Light, the Light of
abundant supply of Divine wealth,
It now releases from the Divine
Intelligence and
Pours over me whose soul is one with
Divine Intelligence.
I now have the power to draw the
permanent abundance to
Expand My Divine Designed Life.
I now attune my consciousness with
Divine Intelligence.
I now expand my vision to see the
Divine gift.
I now command, I now demand
permanent abundance.
It is now manifested; it is now mine
by Divine Right!

Recite above GAM daily for an abundant life.

# GAM TO BE A DYNAMIC AND CHARISMATIC BEING

It is now time to release the dynamic energy from the Divine phase of your mind by awakening the essence within, relaxing daily, reciting the Golden Alchemical Mantra(s) for transmuting your inner and outer conditions that magnify its power:

> **"I am the Divine Essence,**
> **I am the Divine Radiance,**
> **I am the Divine Magnificence!"**

> **"I am the Divine Alpha and Omega,**
> **I am the Divine Omniscence**
> **And Transcendence!"**

Glide your attention from the crown of your head to the tip of your toes as you invoke this **GAM**. You will soon release the transcending power of the supreme resources into your life and affairs. A higher intelligence does the work in your psycho/physical and affairs. It will show you how to live every phase of your life in a dynamic and charismatic way. Integrate into visualization.

# GAM FOR AN ETERNAL YOUTH AND LIFE

The mystic traditions in all ages infer that we have the power to impress the subconscious mind with the image of eternal youth, eternal life and even death itself can be overcome. Recite the following **GAM** daily and integrate it into visualization for further magnifying and enforcing its power.

> **"I am the Divine Eternal Life,**
> **I am the Divine Eternal Youth,**
> **I am the Divine Eternal Energy;**
> **Ageless, Deathless Expression**
> **Of Infinite Being!"**

# Restoration of the Vital Essence

## and Longevity
### An Ancient Golden Alchemical Chant
### (Invocation)

Purple is the color of spirituality and it is an important Alchemical color for peace and healing. It is considered significant as the color gold, an essence of Alchemy. It is a deeply restorative color, helping people to recover from the times of low energy or stress. Purple is associated with the energy of the vital essence; also, it can penetrate into the deeper levels of the subconscious mind and act as a neutralizer on the Karmic substances. Realizing the power of the Purple color, this can transmute the psychological, physical, and emotional problems into a beatific state of mind and conditions.

## Visualization

First relax, become quiet for a moment and gently close your eyes. As you do, consciously

close off the outer vibrations. Visualize the **P**urple
Light being fixed over your head, shining down and
beaming down on you; it enters your body at the
crown of your head all the way down to your feet, and
slowly fills and permeates your body as though you
are immersed in **P**urple **L**ight.

## **C**hant:

> "**I** have **B**ecome the **E**ssence of **P**urple
>
> **L**ight and **V**itality,
> The **P**urple **Q**I of **R**estoration of **H**ealth
> and **L**ongevity. **S**o be it!"

# GAM FOR HEALING:
## Recurring, Hereditary (Karmic) Health Issues

Mystics of all ages explain what is behind all human misery; the various scriptures and doctrines of the world are filled with those subject. They agree that the root of all misery boils down to one's selfish motives and deeds. According to the Karmic Law (the Law of Cause and Effect), one who plants the seed of misery will bear a fruit of misery in this life or the next. The myth of human misery perhaps goes back as far as the story of Genesis.

The Karmic Law will be applied to every human being. Wherever there is an effect, there will always be a cause. If affirmative or negative events become conditions in your subconscious mind, these energies will attract like energy into like result and will simply repeat itself as a merry-go-round until you cut the chain of causation. Law and Order exist above and below. If you violate the Divine Law, you violate the entire system and it causes a short circuit. The transgressor will catch up on your own debts sooner or later. However, the taxation of the original debts will soon accumulate into a mountainous debt. Thus, the penalty can be irreversible. Even the lesser Gods and Angels will be punished and dumped into the dungeon. One who acts selfishly, or does not release the dark emotions of hatred, resentment, fear, and jealousy, is further planting seeds endlessly; this continuously feeds oneself with dark rotten fruit. Eventually, one becomes the rotten fruit itself.

According to the scripture, throwing one's condemnation, curse, or harsh criticism is like hitting a person with an ax, wounding them with a sword, or shooting them with a sharp arrow. All of these weapons will eventually be returned to the sender with multiple forces, which will harm the sender far more than one who inflicted them. The statement of, "Love your enemies who drive you nuts or even drive you to insanity" seems to belong to only those who are enlightened. If you are not accustomed to the Divine Law would say, "You must be joking!" But even this attitude will almost instantly be replaced by reciting the powerful **GAM**(s). You will realize that the attacks of criticism will instantly subside and cease by themselves altogether.

Through the instantaneous, transmutable purifying power, all the disharmonious and destructive conditions will be neutralized and transformed into a beatific state of mind and affairs. In the case of vindicating, condemning someone, immediately recite the **GAM**(s), and that will cease any negative essence from influencing or further building a karmic cause in your subconscious.

> **"I am the Divine Law and Grace,**
> **I am the Divine Conscious**
> **And Subconscious,**
> **I am the Divine Purification**
> **And Transformation!"**

Do everything you can to dissolve the negativities in your subconscious or they will further link to negative things, people and affairs incessantly causing unpleasant experiences to be surfaced on your path. Allow the **G**olden **A**lchemical **M**antra as a base for developing the Divine power within for your advantage. Paracelsus states, "Good thoughts, good words, good deeds help maintain good psychological, physiological, and emotional conditions." *It is a man's kindly acts that are remembered of him in the years after his life (Ptah-hotep).* Therefore, continue planting a seed of peace and harmony; it is the foundation of long lasting success and fulfillment. Integrate into visualization.

# GAM FOR THE HEALING POWER OF LIGHT

*Where the Light is Brightest,*
*the Shadows are Darkest.*

**Goethe**

As the greatest fifteenth century physician and Alchemist, Paracelsus, explained: "Everything that lives lives in light; everything that has an existence radiates light. All things that derive their life from light and this light, in its root are life itself." By sensory perceptions, we are brought into contact with the inner light. We must be aware that tenebrous emotions can dim inner light. The more the inner light is obscured by it, the more it has a chance of conceiving a malignant growth in the body. It is of utmost importance to transmute these emotions into brilliant Divine essence for the greater results.

**"I am the Divine Light and Radiance,**
**I am the Divine Essence And Magnificence!"**

Reciting this daily will stimulate all the atomic energy within your body as though you have become a light being which can transcend all the limitations of the world.  It is said, **"Be ye transformed yourself by renewing of your mind."**  Reciting the **GAM** is to nourish and invigorate the Divine essence within. The statement of "I am the resurrection and the life" can be manifested if it is done properly and the fact has been proven to be true through various historical personages in the world. Recite the following **GAM** daily.

> **"I am the Divine Resurrection,**
> **I am the Divine Ascension,**
> **I am the Divine Illimitable Light**
> **Of the World, Manifest Perfection**
> **Of Being!"**

Life signifies action; lifeless functions can quickly be restored into lively function, so that you can easily accept any challenges in life by awakening the Divine power within.  Recite daily:

> **"I am the Divine Essence and**
> **Vitality,**
> **I am the Divine Action and**
> **Perfection!"**

You will soon feel a new surge of zeal and enthusiasm that will well up within.  Recite the GAM that suite you the best and  integrate into visualization.

# GAM for Golden Blessing
## An Ancient Alchemical Chant
### Invocation

Gold is the most important Alchemical color, since gold transforms adverse emotions such as worry, anger and judgmental attitudes into the gold of healing power. Gold is a symbol of enlightenment, wisdom, and the elixir of immortality.

The Golden Light of invocation was originally an ancient chant conferring "Light" "blessings" and "protection from evil forces." The inner divine radiance is invincible power and dissolves anything that is not divinely planned. It dissolves all appearance of adverse conditions: disease, lack, deprivation or any weapon that is formed against physical harm.

## Visualization

First relax, become quiet for a moment and gently close your eyes. As you do, consciously close off the outer vibrations. Visualize that the luminous

Golden Light is suffusing, sparkling down on you, embracing and filling your body with Gold, letting yourself grow lighter and lighter. Visualize your soul as a magnificent Golden Light shining through every level of being.

## Chant:

"I pray fully to the ruler of heaven to all sacred beings who possess the golden light.

I now command the perennial wisdom, penetrating intelligence quickly to manifest

And protect the true seeker. Divine Intelligence, I now command the Golden Light

To descend. So be it!"

**Reciting sacred texts millions of times develops in the body a clear brilliance and transcends into divine soul.

# GAM FOR
# PHILANTHROPIC LOVE

The statement, "Love one another," is the greatest of all remedies. It goes beyond the Law of Punishment but crowned with the Law of Grace. It is the Divine Panacea that nourishes, heals, restores, and prevails in every aspects of life. It also renews your age and beauty significantly, and it brings forth life, even changing thoughts of death to thoughts of life. With genuine love and temperance, all things are possible; it will purify the entire psychic nature. A life so integrated and so dedicated cannot come to dammed days, nor can it fail in the accomplishment of all things possible to you. The realization is that the power of love produces a great aura of protection and destroys the opponent's dark intentions, whose arrows then become the sweet fragrance of roses. Love and goodwill of the Divine essence are invaluable human qualities. Recite the **GAM** daily to capture the magnificent power. Integrate the following mantra into visualization.

> **"I am the Divine Love and Harmony,**
> **I am the Divine Illimitable Light and Healing,**
> **I am the Supreme Law of Divine Grace!"**

# THE LAW OF KARMA:
# The Secret Law of Gain and Loss

*Things and actions are what they are,*
*And the consequences of them will be*
*What they will be. Why then should we*
*Desire to be deceived?*

**Bishop Joseph Butler**

*T*he aspect of Karma is explained
elaborately in many religious doctrines for centuries;
this seemingly simplistic yet profoundly complex
essence to be captured. This ultimate Law of Gain
and Loss helps readers to understand about the
fundamental concepts and principles of how the Law
operates. Life-long misery and suffering can be
terminated by the Alchemical Dissolution of Karma
Remedy to **"VOID"** your outstanding Karmic debts
and escape from this Law. Furthermore, the chain of
causation can be cut and you can be immune to the

Law of Karma entirely. You can bid farewell to your misery and sufferings forever.

The Law of Karma provides a rational explanation on imbalanced levels of circumstances. The scripture states, **"Whatsoever a man soweth, that shall he also reap,"** or **"As you give, so shall you receive."** Whatever you give to another, in truth, you are giving (input) and sharing (output) with another extension of yourself. If the positive energy returns, you see positive things enter into your life that will cause greater success and happiness to be demonstrated in the outer life. Similarly, if energy has been negatively used to its source, the same source of energy returns to the sender but will almost always returns with the multiplied forces; consequently, it harms the sender the most. Fruition of Karma most often occurs in the same lifetime but in some cases can overflow into another lifetime through the subconscious memory, the memory of incarnation.

This is the time to justify and dissolve outstanding Karmic debts (challenges). If you neglect to treat them, they collect and calcify into your psycho, physical conditions and inconsequence, will reflect on your affairs.

# How to Dissolve Karmic Substance

Is there a solution to the already existing Karmic substance, and, if so, how can you prevent it from further regeneration?  Recalling a past life is not something to be taken lightly, since these records of the subconscious memory are causing you pain and misery and forever binding you to the roots of an ancient Karmic energy.  It seems one's Karmic-substance is indissolvable, as though it is forever intact in the memory bank (subconscious) and comes around for time to time to remind you of your debts.  The Karmic Law of Return is an invincible Divine Law and order; Divine justice does not fail and it seems inescapable since it often paralyzes your world.  There is only one solution to the problem; you must cut the chain of causation to be immune from the Divine Law of Karma forever.

This powerful dissolution remedy can be applied whenever, wherever as much as you need to sustain your life with affirmative ideas and attitude.  The recitation of **GAM** will cause deeper penetration to the lair of its incarnated Karmic essence; however, some of the Karmic-traits are rather tenacious due to their deeply rooted presence in the subconscious.  A successful completion of this process will free you from life-long emotional torment, misfortune, misery and all other cause of unhappiness brought by the Law of Karma: the wall of imprisonment.

Negative thoughts are restless and hard working substances; they easily creep into the mind and dominate the subconscious. Therefore, we must purge all our undesirable traits from the subconscious through the **GAM** daily and it will magnify further the power of its essence.

In order to see the golden harvest of victory and fulfillment in your life, you must plant the seed of the Divine idea in cultivated fertile ground. The **GAM** is the perfect solution for nurturing your desired seed adequately and by reciting **GAM** daily, integrating with visualization is to accelerate the manifestation process of your desires into tangible form. If you neglect the purging process before you plant your desired seeds, your worst traits will highly likely be amplified. In the worst case, tenebrous emotions can absorb your affirmative traits and become a dominant power; they can disrupt the entire acquisition process and result in unfruitful outcome or complete failure. Reciting on the seeds of the Divine designed idea is proven to be the most effective alternative to see the golden harvest. Many times, because of earthly affinities, the additional boost of power that is produced as the result of experimentation will make a magnet out of the negatives, even when they are completely involved in the divine search; inconsequence, it will further link to negative elements and people.

Once the dark Karmic substance is treated from the subconscious, the transformation comes quickly to your full potential. Any belief in restriction or limitation should now be emancipated from the subconscious. The way of the sage is to expect everything directly from the universe, or super-conscious into conscious and subconscious.

# Gam for the Dissolution of Karma

## Preparation

List all the Karmic issues that come around time to time as recurrent bad dreams, haunting and tormenting your life: events, conditions, certain types of people (including the inherent disease that runs in your family). **Throughout the process, keep focusing on the 7th Chakra--at the crown of your head.** As soon as you become accustomed to it, you begin to feel a very gentle electric current of magnetic energy throughout your body.

## Procedure

First, relax, become quiet for a moment. When you are ready, invoke the most powerful Divine protective source of Purple Light.

> **"I invoke the Purple Light**
> **Of the Most High,**
> **Expanding Fire Breath**
> **Of Divine Intelligence!"**

Concentrate on the karmic issues and bring those memories into process. When it is finished, recite the **GAM (s):**

> **"I am the Divine Resurrection,**
> **I am the Divine Manifestation,**
> **I am the Divine Perfect Expression**
> **Of Being!"**

> **"I am the Divine Law and Order,**
> **I am the Divine Justice and Grace,**
> **I now Cut the Chain of Causation.**
> **I am now Immune to the Law**
> **Of Karma!"**

Cease this programming by saying **"So be it"** to enforce the power of the Divine **GAM**.

There is no need to repeat this procedure once you have restored your perfect inner peace. However, heavy Karmic issues are tenacious and lingering since they have strength in their roots. The maximum result is established through your full conviction, a deep and rich connection with the macro cosmic energy of Supreme Intelligence, so that you feel a "click," which is an affirmative energy of the dissolution of Karma; thus, the repetitive application is the key which will intensify and maximize the power of its **GAM**. It starts working on your issues immediately to produce a favorable result. The moment you apply it, it becomes your *mana* (**the Golden Bough**) so as to manifest a miracle in your life. The more you apply this process, the more your can shake the ground and soon an ancient tower of Babel (Karma) will be level ground. As your vision and thinking become clearer, you will be able to enjoy genuine peace and harmony that life is truly joyful. Now you are ready to spring up into the endless avenues of unlimited opportunities.

# Dissolution of Dark Emotions - 1

Psycho/emotional stress arises from human interactions and such emotions of repugnance, indignation, and deplore are simply poisonous in every aspect of life. They often interrupt your higher psychic energy that emerge significant deferment and suspension of good. If nothing negative exists to hold you back, strong factors will automatically surface as your mind will be more concentrated on good. Countless number of people inadvertently programm themselves with an ideas of tribulation and keep visualizing until they are manifested in tangible form. You must supplant all the stigmatized ideas in your subconscious with success, and fulfilling ideas. When you are able to emancipate tenebrous memories, natural healing occurs in the conscious and subconscious level. Recite the **GAM** daily and generate transmutation. Integrate them into visualization for an optimum results .

> **"I am the Divine Conscious,**
> **I am the Divine Subconscious,**
> **I am the Divine Superconscious,**
> **I am the Absolute Affirmative,**
> **Constructive Expression of Being!"**

"I am the Divine Law and Grace,
I am the Divine Love and Wisdom
Manifests through me Every
Where!"

# Dissolution of Dark
## emotions - 2
## Fear, Doubt, and Jealousy

Every love affair generates trepidation, suspicion and jealousy, which they become a chain of reaction. As eclipse overcasts emotions they often bring contradictory conditions in life. These are the worst foe of love, particularly jealously is a Champion among these emotions that is tenaciously ingrained in one's Karmic loam, constantly crucifying and tormenting the self and others. This too, can be eradicated from the root by accustom to the mechanics of the Divine Law and reciting the **Golden Alchemical Mantra** that will inundate the subconscious with constructive elements. It creates new prospects, and develops a foundation for panache and superlative ideas into life. Daily reciting the **GAM** will optimize its power; integrate into visualization. Thus, everything will become quiet and peaceful.

**"I am the Divine Conscious,
I am the Divine Subconscious,
I am the Divine Superconscious!"**

"I am the Divine Essence,
I am the Divine Radiance,
I am the Divine Magnificence!"

"I am the Divine Law and Order,
I am the Divine Justice,
I am the Divine Grace!"

When you emancipate the object, it will automatically lose its intensity. Similarly, if you do not nourish your ego with egocentric thoughts, it will not propagate by itself. When you are no longer disturbed by opponents' cruelty, he/she will cease to be cruel. The Law of Polarity assures its mechanism.

# DISSOLUTION OF
# MALIGNANT GROWTH

According to the Law of Karma, almost all malignant growths in the body are nourished by the result of active dreadful memories. It is like an active volcano ready to burst its pus. The Law of Like Attracts Like denotes that nourishing your mind with healthy life-giving thoughts will generate pristine cells in your body. With a lack of sustenance, the roots of all disease, including malignant growth in the body, will soon lose their vehemence to come out of their crux. In addition to visualization, recite the **GAM** daily until perfect transmutation occurs in your subconscious to secure an alternate, desirable conscious mind and attitude.

**"I am the Divine Law and Grace,**
**I am the Divine Body, Mind, and Soul,**
  **Ageless, Deathless Expression**
  **Of Infinite Being!"**

**"I am the Divine Ever-Regenerating,**
  **Ever-Rejuvenating,**
  **Ever-Illuminating Divine Fountain;**
  **Ageless, Deathless Expression**
  **Of Divine Essence!"**

# *List of Illustrations*

# *B*ibliography

| | |
|---|---|
| Achille B. | *Symbolicae Quaestiones,* London, 1574. |
| Allmen, J. J. Von | A Companion to the Bible. Oxford University Press, New York, 1958 |
| Archer-Hid, R. D. | *Plato's Cosmology.* Kegan Paul, 1935. |
| Buret, J. trans. | *The Works of Plato.* O.U. Press, 3rd ed. 1892. |
| Betwih, N. | *Philo Judaeus of Alexadria.* Philadelphia, 1910. |
| Blavatsky, H. P. | *The Secret Doctrine,* Adyar: Theosophical Publishing House, 1938, 4th ed., vol. 2, p.359. |
| Box, H. | *Philonis Alexandrini in Flaccum.* London and New York, 1939. |
| Bradbury, W. | *Into the Unknown.* Reader's Digest Association Ltd. Canada, 1981 |
| Burckhardt, T. | *Alchemy,* Penguin Books, Baltimore, 1971. |

| | |
|---|---|
| Campbell, J. | *The Power of Myth. (Interview with B. Moyers)*, Doubleday: New York. |
| Capra, F. | *The Tao of Physics*, Shambhala Publications: Berkeley, 1975. |
| Crowley, A. | *The Book of Thoth*, Weiser, New York, 1969. |
| Cumont, F. | *Astrology and Religion among the Greeks and Romans.* New York, 1912. *The Oriental Religions in Roman Paganism.* Chicago, 1911. |
| Deissmann, A. | *Light from the Ancient East.* Revised edition. London, 1922. |
| Doresse, J. | *The Secret Books of the Egyptian Gnostics.* New York, 1960. |
| Gaddis, V. H. | *Mysterious Fires and Lights.* Dell: New York, 1967. |
| Goodenough, E. R. | *By Light, Light; the Mystic Gospel of Hellenistic Judaism.* Oxford, 1935. |
| Grant, R. M. | Gnostiism: *A Source of Heretial Writings.* New York, 1961. |

Grunbaum, A.      *Philosophical Problems of Space and Time.* D. Reidel: Boston, 1973.

Jeffe, A.      *The Myth of Meaning.* Hodder and Stoughton: London, 1970.

Hanson, V.      *Karma, The Universal Law of Harmon.* Theosophical Publishing House, 1981

Herbert, N.      *Faster Than Light.* New York: New American Library, 1988.

Heelan, P. A.      *Quantum Mechanics and Objectivity.* Martinus Nijhoff: The Hague, 1965.

Jeans, J. Sir.      *The Mysterious Universe.* E. P. Dutton, New York, 1932.

Jonas, H.      *The Gnostic Religion: The Message of the Alien God and the Beginning Of Christianity.* Beacon Press, Boston, 1958

Katz, P.      *Philo's Bible.* Cambridge, 1950

King, F.     *Ritual Magic in England.* Spearman, London, 1970 *Astral Projection, Magic and Alchemy, Spearman.* London, 1971

Moorsel, G. van.     *The Mysteries of Hermes Trismegistos.* Utrecht, 1955

Oakley, Cooper I.     *The Comte de St. Germain. Milan, 1912*

Panchadasi, Swami.     *The Astral World.* Delhi, India, 1921.

Redgrove, H. S.,     *Alchemy: Ancient and Modern, Rider.* London, 1922

Ryle, H.E.     *Philo ad Holy Scripture.* London & New York, 1895

Sagan, C.     *The Cosmic Connection.* Dell: New York, 1973.

Sarfatti, J. & Toben. B.     *Space-Time and Beyond.* E. P. Dutton: New York, 1975.

Schwartz, L.     *Juxtaposition of Leonardo's Self-portrait and Mona Lisa.* New York, 1998

Sri Aurobindo.     *A legend and a symbol* Sri Aurobindo Ashram Press: Pondicherry, 1954

Walker, B.

*Gnosticism: Its History and Influence.* Aquarian Press, Wellingborough, 1983

Whitehead, A. N.

*The Concept of Nature.* Macmillan: New York, 1925.

Whittaker, Sir E.

*Space and Spirit.* Regnery: Hinsdale, Ill., 1948.

# About the Author

She is the author of nationally recognized book *Great Alchemist and Quantum Manifestation Power: St. Germain's Secret Alchemical Remedy for Victory and Fulfillment.*

Her principal studies are in Psychology, Oriental Medicine, and Ministerial Religious Education. She received her Master's and Doctoral degrees in Counseling Psychology, Pastoral Counseling Psychology, Mythological Psychology, Ministry, Oriental Medicine, Anthropology and Science Education.

Printed in Great Britain
by Amazon

76713040R00078